Jellybean Books™

TRUCKS

By Harry McNaught

Random House New York

D1275387

Whirrr, whirrr goes the fire engine as it races through the streets. The siren warns people to get out of the way when the fire engine is rushing to a fire.

Fire engines have ladders and hoses attached to them. They help the firefighters reach the top floors of buildings and put out fires.

When there are no fires, the firefighters clean the trucks and get ready for the next alarm.

What else do trucks do?
Trucks carry heavy loads!

This is a dump truck. It carries dirt and rocks. This one can carry 85 tons. That's as much as 17 elephants weigh!

These trucks carry trees. First the log loader picks up the logs and stacks them.

Then the big tractor-trailer carries the logs to the lumber mill, where they will be cut into boards. What would we do without trucks?

Buses are trucks, too. They carry people.

Can you imagine riding on the second story of a bus—and looking *down* on all the other cars and trucks! You could if you lived in a city with double-decker buses, like London, England.

School buses are another kind of bus. You have probably seen them where you live. School buses are usually bright yellow. They take children to school and back.

Here is a truck made just for carrying
other trucks!

How many trucks can you count?

What do trucks do besides carry things?
Trucks make new roads!

This tractor hauls away dirt. Then
other trucks make the new road smooth
and even.

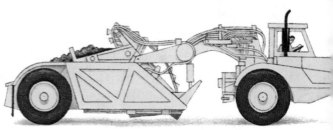

ELEVATING SCRAPER

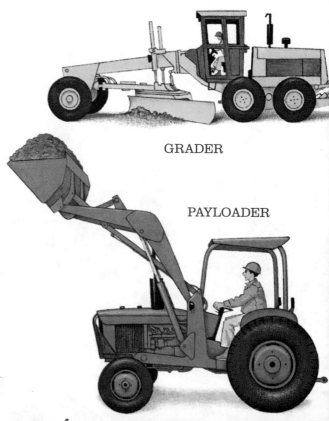

GRADER

PAYLOADER

Trucks also help make buildings.
Cranes lift beams and pipes up in
the air, to the very top floors
of tall buildings.

This truck mixes concrete and pours it out to make sidewalks, floors, and the foundations of buildings.

Trucks help people in many ways, but these trucks are just for fun! People take vacations in them. Some of them are so big that they have their own bathrooms and kitchens!

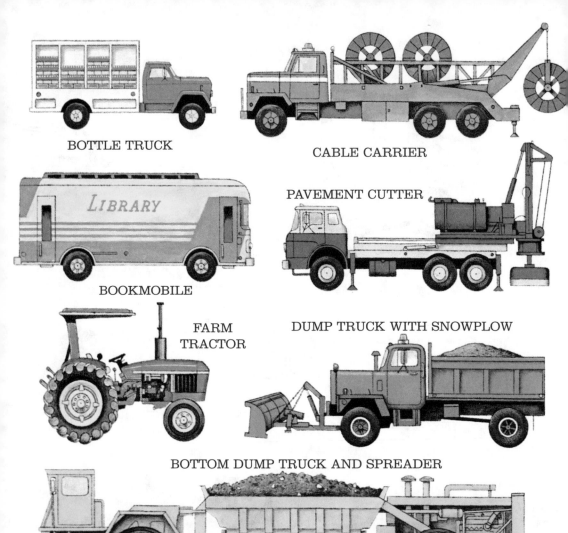

BOTTLE TRUCK

CABLE CARRIER

LIBRARY

BOOKMOBILE

PAVEMENT CUTTER

FARM TRACTOR

DUMP TRUCK WITH SNOWPLOW

BOTTOM DUMP TRUCK AND SPREADER

TRACTOR-TRAILER WITH CAB UNDERNEATH

There are all sorts of different trucks in the world, and they do many important jobs.

Almost everywhere you go, trucks are hard at work.

GLAZIER'S TRUCK

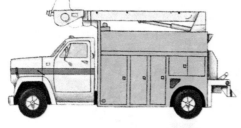

TELEPHONE POLE PLANTER

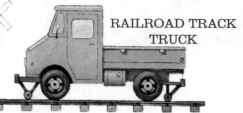

RAILROAD TRACK TRUCK

HIGH-LIFT TRUCK

EARLY ELECTRIC TRUCK

MODEL-T FIRE ENGINE

And it's been that way for a long, long time.

FIFTH AVENUE BUS, NEW YORK CITY